This Dream Journal Belongs To:

_____

Meaning of Common Dreams

Falling
- It likely means that a recent choice or situation has made you anxious. More so if you're being overcome with fear in your dream.
- If you feel happy while falling, it suggests that you welcome recent changes and are ready to embrace them.
- If you're falling into the water, it may mean that you have strong feelings for someone.

Your teeth fell out
- You are anxious about your appearance or attractiveness. These dreams may stem from a fear of rejection.
- It might also mean an inability to express yourself or communicate with someone. Generally, losing teeth means losing confidence.

Being chased in a dream
- It suggests that you're avoiding something in daily life.
- You are trying to escape your fears or desires.
- To understand this dream better, it may be necessary to know who is chasing you. If you're being chased by an animal, you are running away from your own emotions. If the pursuer is unknown, you may be running away from past trauma. If the pursuer is of the gender you're attracted to, it may mean you have hangups about love, relationships, and sex.

Dying

- It may suggest that you are facing a big change in your life.
- It may also mean fear of inevitable change--your children growing up, you getting old.
- It may also suggest that you are processing the inevitable death of a sick loved one. And since "the other side" is unknown, our subconscious processes it into something more meaningful. It may mean dreaming of a loved one, or of dying yourself as you evolve into something else.

Dreaming that you can't find the toilet

- There's a joke that if you find a toilet in a dream, don't use it: it's a trap. But what if you can't find the toilet. It may mean that you're having difficulty expressing your needs in certain situations.

Dreams about being unprepared or failing a test

- It usually suggests fear of failing.
- It may mean a lack of confidence in the next stages of your life.
- This type of dream is common to adolescents, but may also appear to adults who are facing imminent change.

Flying

- If you're having difficulty flying in your dream, it may mean that there's an obstacle facing you as you move to the next phase of your life.
- If you're happily and skillfully flying, it may mean that you are enjoying your freedom, independence, or current state of your life.

 # Dream Journal

Date ——————————— Time ———————————

Your thoughts before going to bed

_____
_____
_____
_____

Your feelings before going to bed

_____
_____
_____
_____

Your Dreams   In Color? ———————

_____
_____
_____
_____
_____

Your Interpretation

_____
_____
_____
_____

 # Dream Journal

Date ——————— Time ———————

Your thoughts before going to bed

_____
_____
_____
_____

Your feelings before going to bed

_____
_____
_____
_____

Your Dreams   In Color? ———————

_____
_____
_____
_____
_____

Your Interpretation

_____
_____
_____
_____

Dream Journal

Date ———————— Time ————————

Your thoughts before going to bed

Your feelings before going to bed

Your Dreams   In Color? ————————

Your Interpretation

Dream Journal

Date _____ Time _____

Your thoughts before going to bed

_____
_____
_____

Your feelings before going to bed

_____
_____
_____

Your Dreams   In Color?

_____
_____
_____

Your Interpretation

_____
_____
_____
_____

Dream Journal

Date _____ Time _____

Your thoughts before going to bed

_____
_____
_____
_____

Your feelings before going to bed

_____
_____
_____
_____

Your Dreams   In Color?

_____
_____
_____
_____
_____

Your Interpretation

_____
_____
_____
_____

Dream Journal

Date _____ Time _____

Your thoughts before going to bed

_____
_____
_____
_____

Your feelings before going to bed

_____
_____
_____
_____

Your Dreams   In Color? _____

_____
_____
_____
_____
_____

Your Interpretation

_____
_____
_____
_____

Dream Journal

Date ——————————— Time ———————————

Your thoughts before going to bed

_____
_____
_____
_____

Your feelings before going to bed

_____
_____
_____

Your Dreams   In Color? ———————————

_____
_____
_____
_____

Your Interpretation

_____
_____
_____
_____

 # Dream Journal

Date _____ Time _____

Your thoughts before going to bed

_____

_____

_____

_____

Your feelings before going to bed

_____

_____

_____

_____

Your Dreams   In Color? _____

_____

_____

_____

_____

_____

Your Interpretation

_____

_____

_____

_____

Dream Journal

Date _____   Time _____

Your thoughts before going to bed

_____
_____
_____
_____

Your feelings before going to bed

_____
_____
_____
_____

Your Dreams   In Color? _____

_____
_____
_____
_____
_____
_____

Your Interpretation

_____
_____
_____
_____

 # Dream Journal

Date ———————————— Time ————————————

Your thoughts before going to bed

_____

_____

_____

_____

Your feelings before going to bed

_____

_____

_____

_____

Your Dreams   In Color? ————————

_____

_____

_____

_____

_____

Your Interpretation

_____

_____

_____

_____

Dream Journal

Date ——————— Time ———————

Your thoughts before going to bed

_____

_____

_____

_____

Your feelings before going to bed

_____

_____

_____

_____

Your Dreams   In Color? ———————

_____

_____

_____

_____

Your Interpretation

_____

_____

_____

_____

Dream Journal

Date ————————— Time —————————

Your thoughts before going to bed

_____
_____
_____
_____

Your feelings before going to bed

_____
_____
_____
_____

Your Dreams   In Color? —————————
_____
_____
_____
_____
_____

Your Interpretation

_____
_____
_____
_____

Dream Journal

Date _____   Time _____

Your thoughts before going to bed

_____
_____
_____
_____

Your feelings before going to bed

_____
_____
_____

Your Dreams   **In Color?** _____

_____
_____
_____
_____
_____

Your Interpretation

_____
_____
_____
_____

Dream Journal

Date _____   Time _____

Your thoughts before going to bed

_____

_____

_____

_____

Your feelings before going to bed

_____

_____

_____

_____

Your Dreams   In Color? _____

_____

_____

_____

_____

Your Interpretation

_____

_____

_____

_____

 # Dream Journal

Date _____   Time _____

Your thoughts before going to bed

_____
_____
_____
_____

Your feelings before going to bed

_____
_____
_____
_____

Your Dreams   In Color? _____

_____
_____
_____
_____

Your Interpretation

_____
_____
_____
_____

 # Dream Journal

Date ——————— Time ———————

Your thoughts before going to bed

————————————————————————————
————————————————————————————
————————————————————————————
————————————————————————————

Your feelings before going to bed

————————————————————————————
————————————————————————————
————————————————————————————
————————————————————————————

Your Dreams   In Color? ———————

————————————————————————————
————————————————————————————
————————————————————————————
————————————————————————————
————————————————————————————

Your Interpretation

————————————————————————————
————————————————————————————
————————————————————————————
————————————————————————————

Dream Journal

Date _____ Time _____

Your thoughts before going to bed

_____

_____

_____

_____

Your feelings before going to bed

_____

_____

_____

_____

Your Dreams   In Color? _____

_____

_____

_____

_____

Your Interpretation

_____

_____

_____

_____

Dream Journal

Date .... Time ....

Your thoughts before going to bed

....
....
....
....

Your feelings before going to bed

....
....
....
....

Your Dreams   In Color? ....

....
....
....
....
....
....

Your Interpretation

....
....
....
....

Dream Journal

Date ⎯⎯⎯⎯⎯⎯ Time ⎯⎯⎯⎯⎯⎯

Your thoughts before going to bed

Your feelings before going to bed

Your Dreams   In Color? ⎯⎯⎯⎯

Your Interpretation

Dream Journal

Date _____   Time _____

Your thoughts before going to bed

_____

_____

_____

_____

Your feelings before going to bed

_____

_____

_____

_____

Your Dreams   In Color? _____

_____

_____

_____

_____

Your Interpretation

_____

_____

_____

_____

Dream Journal

Date _____   Time _____

Your thoughts before going to bed

_____

_____

_____

_____

Your feelings before going to bed

_____

_____

_____

_____

Your Dreams   In Color? _____

_____

_____

_____

_____

Your Interpretation

_____

_____

_____

_____

 # Dream Journal

Date _____ Time _____

Your thoughts before going to bed

_____

_____

_____

_____

Your feelings before going to bed

_____

_____

_____

_____

Your Dreams   In Color? _____

_____

_____

_____

_____

_____

Your Interpretation

_____

_____

_____

_____

 # Dream Journal

Date _____   Time _____

Your thoughts before going to bed

_____

_____

_____

_____

Your feelings before going to bed

_____

_____

_____

Your Dreams   In Color? _____

_____

_____

_____

_____

Your Interpretation

_____

_____

_____

_____

Dream Journal

Date _____ Time _____

Your thoughts before going to bed

_____
_____
_____
_____

Your feelings before going to bed

_____
_____
_____
_____

Your Dreams   In Color? _____

_____
_____
_____
_____
_____
_____

Your Interpretation

_____
_____
_____
_____

 # Dream Journal

Date _____   Time _____

Your thoughts before going to bed

_____
_____
_____
_____

Your feelings before going to bed

_____
_____
_____
_____

Your Dreams   In Color? _____

_____
_____
_____
_____
_____

Your Interpretation

_____
_____
_____
_____

Dream Journal

Date _____   Time _____

Your thoughts before going to bed

_____
_____
_____
_____

Your feelings before going to bed

_____
_____
_____
_____

Your Dreams   In Color? _____

_____
_____
_____
_____

Your Interpretation

_____
_____
_____
_____

Dream Journal

Date _____   Time _____

Your thoughts before going to bed

_____
_____
_____
_____

Your feelings before going to bed

_____
_____
_____
_____

Your Dreams   In Color? _____

_____
_____
_____
_____
_____
_____

Your Interpretation

_____
_____
_____
_____

Dream Journal

Date _____ Time _____

Your thoughts before going to bed

_____
_____
_____

Your feelings before going to bed

_____
_____
_____
_____

Your Dreams   In Color? _____

_____
_____
_____
_____

Your Interpretation

_____
_____
_____
_____

Dream Journal

Date _____   Time _____

Your thoughts before going to bed

_____

_____

_____

_____

Your feelings before going to bed

_____

_____

_____

Your Dreams   In Color? _____

_____

_____

_____

_____

Your Interpretation

_____

_____

_____

_____

Dream Journal

Date _____   Time _____

Your thoughts before going to bed

_____
_____
_____
_____

Your feelings before going to bed

_____
_____
_____
_____

Your Dreams   In Color? _____

_____
_____
_____
_____
_____

Your Interpretation

_____
_____
_____
_____

Dream Journal

Date _____   Time _____

Your thoughts before going to bed

_____
_____
_____
_____

Your feelings before going to bed

_____
_____
_____
_____

Your Dreams   In Color? _____

_____
_____
_____
_____
_____
_____

Your Interpretation

_____
_____
_____
_____

Dream Journal

Date _____ Time _____

Your thoughts before going to bed

_____
_____
_____

Your feelings before going to bed

_____
_____
_____
_____

Your Dreams   In Color? _____

_____
_____
_____
_____
_____

Your Interpretation

_____
_____
_____
_____

Dream Journal

Date _____   Time _____

Your thoughts before going to bed

_____
_____
_____
_____

Your feelings before going to bed

_____
_____
_____
_____

Your Dreams   In Color? _____

_____
_____
_____
_____
_____

Your Interpretation

_____
_____
_____

Dream Journal

Date _____ Time _____

Your thoughts before going to bed

_____

_____

_____

_____

Your feelings before going to bed

_____

_____

_____

Your Dreams   In Color? _____

_____

_____

_____

_____

Your Interpretation

_____

_____

_____

_____

Dream Journal

Date _____ Time _____

Your thoughts before going to bed

_____
_____
_____
_____

Your feelings before going to bed

_____
_____
_____
_____

Your Dreams   In Color? _____

_____
_____
_____
_____
_____

Your Interpretation

_____
_____
_____
_____

Dream Journal

Date ——————— Time ———————

Your thoughts before going to bed

_____
_____
_____
_____

Your feelings before going to bed

_____
_____
_____

Your Dreams   In Color? ———————

_____
_____
_____
_____
_____

Your Interpretation

_____
_____
_____
_____

Dream Journal

Date _____   Time _____

Your thoughts before going to bed

_____

_____

_____

_____

Your feelings before going to bed

_____

_____

_____

_____

Your Dreams   In Color? _____

_____

_____

_____

_____

_____

Your Interpretation

_____

_____

_____

_____

 # Dream Journal

Date _____   Time _____

Your thoughts before going to bed

_____
_____
_____

Your feelings before going to bed

_____
_____
_____

Your Dreams   In Color?

_____
_____
_____
_____

Your Interpretation

_____
_____
_____

Dream Journal

Date _____ Time _____

Your thoughts before going to bed

_____
_____
_____
_____

Your feelings before going to bed

_____
_____
_____
_____

Your Dreams   In Color? _____

_____
_____
_____
_____
_____

Your Interpretation

_____
_____
_____
_____

 # Dream Journal

Date _____   Time _____

Your thoughts before going to bed

_____

_____

_____

_____

Your feelings before going to bed

_____

_____

_____

_____

Your Dreams   In Color?

_____

_____

_____

_____

_____

Your Interpretation

_____

_____

_____

_____

Dream Journal

Date ———————   Time ———————

Your thoughts before going to bed

———————————————————————
———————————————————————
———————————————————————
———————————————————————

Your feelings before going to bed

———————————————————————
———————————————————————
———————————————————————
———————————————————————

Your Dreams   In Color?

———————————————————————
———————————————————————
———————————————————————
———————————————————————
———————————————————————

Your Interpretation

———————————————————————
———————————————————————
———————————————————————
———————————————————————

Dream Journal

Date _____   Time _____

Your thoughts before going to bed

_____
_____
_____
_____

Your feelings before going to bed

_____
_____
_____
_____

Your Dreams   In Color? _____

_____
_____
_____
_____
_____

Your Interpretation

_____
_____
_____
_____

Dream Journal

Date _____   Time _____

Your thoughts before going to bed

_____

_____

_____

Your feelings before going to bed

_____

_____

_____

Your Dreams   In Color? _____

_____

_____

_____

_____

Your Interpretation

_____

_____

_____

Dream Journal

Date _____   Time _____

Your thoughts before going to bed

_____

_____

_____

_____

Your feelings before going to bed

_____

_____

_____

_____

Your Dreams   In Color? _____

_____

_____

_____

_____

_____

Your Interpretation

_____

_____

_____

_____

 # Dream Journal

Date _____   Time _____

Your thoughts before going to bed

_____

_____

_____

_____

Your feelings before going to bed

_____

_____

_____

_____

Your Dreams   In Color? _____

_____

_____

_____

_____

_____

Your Interpretation

_____

_____

_____

_____

 # Dream Journal

Date _____ Time _____

Your thoughts before going to bed

_____

_____

_____

_____

Your feelings before going to bed

_____

_____

_____

_____

Your Dreams   In Color? _____

_____

_____

_____

_____

_____

Your Interpretation

_____

_____

_____

_____

Dream Journal

Date _____   Time _____

Your thoughts before going to bed

_____
_____
_____
_____

Your feelings before going to bed

_____
_____
_____
_____

Your Dreams   In Color? _____

_____
_____
_____
_____
_____

Your Interpretation

_____
_____
_____
_____

Dream Journal

Date _____   Time _____

Your thoughts before going to bed

_____
_____
_____
_____

Your feelings before going to bed

_____
_____
_____
_____

Your Dreams   In Color? _____

_____
_____
_____
_____
_____

Your Interpretation

_____
_____
_____
_____

Printed in Great Britain
by Amazon

74644440R00032